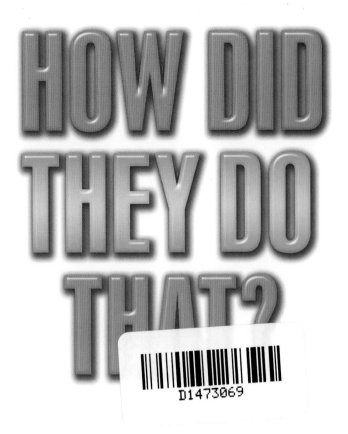

HOW DID THEY DO THAT?

D1473069

Built for SPEED
by Anastasia Suen

Mind-Boggling BRIDGES
by Ellen Dreyer

GLOBE FEARON
Pearson Learning Group

CONTENTS

Built for SPEED

Mind-Boggling BRIDGES

Built for SPEED

by Anastasia Suen

Chapter 1 — Faster, Faster!

Imagine you are in a bicycle race, competing against your friends. You want to be the first to cross the finish line. You pedal faster and faster. Your heart is beating quickly. As you speed downhill, you feel the wind blowing through your hair. You feel like you are moving faster than you've ever moved before. You feel like you are flying.

Since ancient times, humans have raced against each other. They have felt the thrill of pushing the limits, moving faster and faster. Long before people could watch the Olympic Games on television, ancient Greek people took part in athletic competitions. If you look into the past, you can learn how the desire to move quickly has always been important. People have spent a lot of energy and time figuring out how to achieve the fastest speeds possible.

This book selection will take you on a journey to explore the world of speed. Along the way, you will learn about some of the inventions and thoughts that led to creating and improving vehicles so they can move faster and more **efficiently**. You will see how people have always tried to improve on their past speed records, whether they are racing along the ground, on tracks, or in the sky.

Engine Power

Line up your chariots and take your mark, get set, go! Historians think the wheel was first used for moving people and goods in about 3500 BCE. Back then, however, vehicles did not move by their own power. Where did the power come from? Animals, including wild horses and donkeys, did the work, pulling carts and wagons from place to place. Naturally, once people could move from one place to another on wheels, they came up with ways to move faster and faster. They eventually wanted to race to see whose horse and wagon could move the fastest. Picture a noisy, colorful arena in ancient times with horse-drawn chariots lined up at a starting gate, ready to race. That is how formal racing began.

How did we get from animal-drawn vehicles to the shiny racing and sports cars of today? The story of modern vehicles begins with a steam engine. The first successful steam engine was invented at the beginning of the 1700s. This important invention changed the way vehicles moved. For the first time, vehicles could move by themselves instead of relying on animals to pull them.

The first steam engine was invented to solve a **perceived** problem. As coal miners dug underground, the mines often filled with water, creating a safety **hazard**. An English inventor figured out a way to solve this problem. He invented the steam engine to pump water out of the mines. Water was heated to create steam. The force of the steam was powerful. That power could be used as energy to move parts of an engine and pump water deep in the mines to a drain at the top.

In the mid 1700s, Scottish inventor and mechanical engineer James Watt studied the steam engine. One of his **ambitions** was to improve on this invention. He figured out a way to make the engine more **efficient**. Watt made the steam engine much more powerful than it was before.

Watt had improved the steam engine, but he still wasn't satisfied. A steam engine moved a piston up and down. Watt was determined to get the piston to move in a circular motion. He got the piston to move in a circle around an axis, or center point. Once the piston could move that way, a wheel could be hooked up to it and move in a circle, too. As soon as the steam engine could work with a wheel, it was used to power vehicles.

Inventors began to add engines to many kinds of vehicles. An engine could make an amazing difference. Vehicles moved faster than ever. Inventors didn't stop there. Some inventors added more pistons to their engines. Others tried out new fuels, using gasoline instead of coal. Each new change **enabled** vehicles to move faster and better. Beginning with the story of the car, this book will describe how new ideas and creative thinking set the pace and led to increased speed.

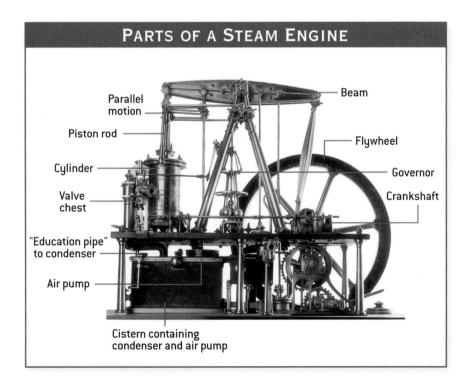

PARTS OF A STEAM ENGINE

Parallel motion

Beam

Piston rod

Cylinder

Flywheel

Valve chest

Governor

Crankshaft

"Education pipe" to condenser

Air pump

Cistern containing condenser and air pump

Chapter 2
Cars Take to the Road

During the 1800s, U.S. citizens and Europeans tried to create a vehicle that did not depend on animals for power. Some inventors attempted to use steam to power their engines. Others turned to hot air or electricity. Some **ambitious** inventors tried to create motors that were more powerful. In the early 1860s, Belgian-born Jean-Joseph-Etienne Lenoir created an **efficient** engine that worked by burning gasoline. Gasoline and air exploded when a spark ignited inside an engine. Lenoir had produced the first practical internal combustion engine. The automobile age had begun.

The first cars were built by hand, one car at a time. Each car took a long time to manufacture. Companies could only make a few cars each year. So cars were expensive. Only wealthy people could afford to buy them. Henry Ford's ideas changed the way cars were manufactured.

In 1913, Ford introduced the idea of the assembly line. Ford had worked on this method of producing cars for several years. What was special about this new method? Before Ford, a small team of workers built one car at a time. In Ford's factory, large teams of workers assembled cars one part at a time. After each worker added a part, the car moved down the production line to the next worker. That worker added another part, and so on until the car was finished.

People realized that Ford's method was a much more **efficient** one. The use of assembly lines meant that cars were built more quickly. Producing cars in this way meant that the prices of cars dropped dramatically. Ford's assembly line made it possible for many people to afford cars. As cars became more common, drivers wanted more power and speed for their vehicles. New cars were developed to run more **efficiently** and faster.

On Your Mark

Soon, drivers wanted to test the limits of their
vehicles. People thought about racing these vehicles,
trying to achieve the highest speeds possible. Early
carmakers began to build race cars. Building race cars
gave carmakers the chance to test new ideas for regular
passenger cars. Inventors and designers studied engines
and body design. If the new design ideas worked well
under racing conditions, these ideas were then put into
use in passenger cars.

By the early 1900s, special tracks were built for racing.
Race cars were designed and built especially to compete at
high speeds. Back then, high speeds were about 75 miles
per hour (mph). Since those early days, peoples' **perceptions**
of what is fast have changed. What is the fastest car in the
world today? The Thrust-Powered SuperSonic Car
(ThrustSSC) is a British-made custom car. If you want to go
for a test drive, you may be disappointed. The ThrustSSC
probably won't appear at a car dealer near your home
anytime soon. This vehicle is equipped with a jet engine!

Jet-powered cars like the ThrustSSC race for only 1
mile, but they can take 6 miles to warm up and 6 miles to
slow down. What kinds of track could you race one of
these cars on? To race that far in a straight line you need
to race in a desert. After many attempts, the ThrustSSC
set a new land speed record. On October 15, 1997, the
ThrustSSC team drove the car at just over 759 mph.
Within an hour, the car completed the return run, at a
speed of just over 766 mph. The ThrustSSC team's
record-breaking speed averaged more than 763 mph.

Speedy Race Cars

In early car races, one assembly-line car competed against another, but racing didn't stay that way for very long. Racers as well as carmakers made improvements to their cars so they could win. Over the years nearly every aspect of the race car changed—both inside and out. Depending upon the type of race a car competes in, cars have different requirements. Racing for a quarter of a mile is far different from racing for 500 miles.

Drag racing takes place between two cars that begin at the same starting line and race side by side. The cars start out in a place called the burnout box. Here, the drivers spin the huge rear wheels of their cars. The spinning results when the drivers press the accelerator and the brake of their car at the same time. Spinning heats up the tires, which improves the tires' traction, or grip on the road. As the yellow lights flash, both cars move forward to begin the race. When the light turns green the race is on!

Drag racers only race for a quarter of a mile. The car that crosses the finish line first wins. The two drag racers drive as fast as they can—more than 300 mph. Drag races are short in distance so speed is everything. How do the cars come to a stop after driving so fast? A parachute comes out of the back of the race car to slow it down. As a **precaution**, each lane has a sand pit at the end. If the parachute doesn't slow it down, the car will run into the sand pit at the end of the lane. The sand will stop the car to avoid the **hazard** of a crash.

Three of the most popular types of cars run in drag races are top-fuel dragsters, funny cars, and pro stock cars. How can you tell the difference? Top-fuel dragsters have huge rear wheels and small front wheels. The length of these cars can be up to 300 inches, or 25 feet. In fact, the cars look like long skinny mechanical insects. Top fuelers are the fastest dragsters in the world!

At first glance, funny cars may look like regular road cars with huge rear wheels. Their bodies often carry advertisements for different companies or sponsors. These cars don't have doors. To get inside a funny car, drivers have to lift up the body of the car and climb inside.

Pro stock cars may look more like regular cars than other dragsters. However, you will never mistake one for a family vehicle. Drag racers have oversized tires and huge air scoops on the front hood. These hood scoops draw in large amounts of air that **enable** the engine to produce greater horsepower.

Stock cars that race in longer races rely on aerodynamics for **maximum** handling and downforce. A car that drives long distances **functions** better when the outside air moves over the car quickly. Most stock cars race on long, oval tracks. The most famous stock car race is the Daytona 500. The track is 2 miles around, so the cars have to do 250 laps to complete this 500-mile race.

One of the best-known race car drivers was Dale Earnhardt. Nicknamed The Intimidator, Earnhardt won nearly every major racing event that he could compete in. Ever since he was a child and watched his own father race stock cars, Earnhardt knew he wanted to race. As a teenager, he worked during the day, and worked on his cars or raced at night. Earnhardt went on to have one of the most successful careers in the history of racing. Sadly, Dale Earnhardt died of head injuries as he took the last turn on the last lap of the Daytona 500 in 2001. His son, driver Dale Earnhardt, Jr., carries on his legacy.

Dale Earnhardt's car is pictured here. Does it look like a typical car on the highway?

Formula Racing: Start Your Engines!

Take one look at the dashboard of a Formula One car, and you might think you are in the cockpit of an airplane. Drivers of these single-seat racing cars need computerized displays and warning lights in order to control their car at high speeds. Formula racing follows a set of rules or formulas. There are many different types of formula races, but the top one is Formula One.

Formula One races are also known as Grand Prix races. Actually, the Grand Prix is a series of races—usually 16. Formula One racing takes place on a long track. Grand Prix tracks have both left and right turns and the straight parts are not equal in length. Designing road courses this way makes the race even more challenging.

Formula One race cars are designed to move quickly in any direction. Drivers can pass one another on winding roads. **Maximum** speed is important on straight parts of the track. In the turns, to prevent **collisions**, agility counts.

Ready to race? This Formula One race car is on track.

Formula One cars can zoom at more than 200 mph. However, the cars must slow down to take the curves. "If you would go for **maximum** speed, you would probably go beyond 500 if you wanted," says race car driver Michael Schumacher. He has been the top Formula One driver in the world seven times.

Schumacher began racing karts when he was four years old. By the age of 18, Schumacher was a race-kart champion. Then, he started racing different levels of formula cars until he graduated to Formula One cars. Why does Schumacher race? "We don't do it for the thrill of the danger. We do it for the thrill of speed."

Motorcycles on the Move

What do you get if you add a motor to a bicycle? A motorcycle. In 1867, U.S. inventor Sylvester Howard Roper put a coal-powered steam engine under a bike seat. Although it had a motor, the bike itself was made of wood. Roper took it to fairs to show people how it worked. Today, you can see Roper's invention in the Smithsonian Institution in Washington, D.C.

In Germany, inventor Gottlieb Daimler tested a different **hypothesis**. He didn't use coal. In 1885, Daimler attached a gasoline motor to a wooden bicycle. The bicycle also had a pair of small wheels under the motor that looked like training wheels. However, a person could run as fast as this motorcycle could move.

Inventors kept trying new **variations**, and eventually came up with a twin-cylinder engine. Using two cylinders instead of one made a huge difference. A twin-cylinder engine motorcycle could move at 24 mph. In 1894 that meant a motorcycle could move faster than most cars.

Once motorcycles could move fast, the idea of motorcycle racing caught on. Like car races, the first motorcycle races were on open roads. This kind of racing turned out to be quite **hazardous**. Drivers crashed on the narrow roads and spectators walked onto the road during the races. After several accidents, the races had to be stopped. As a **precaution**, special racetracks were built for motorcycles.

Like car racing, motorcycle racing has several **variations**. The American Motorcyclist Association (AMA) oversees five different types of motorcycle races: hillclimb, dirt track, supercross/motocross, road racing, and supermoto. Each type of race has **precise** rules about how it is run and which motorcycles may enter. In all motorcycle races, engines of like size race against one another.

Racing Motorcycles

A hillclimb race is just what it sounds like—motorcycles climbing up hills. However, there are two ways to win. In hillclimb races, the motorcycles race either against the clock or for a required distance.

Dirt track racing is also called flat-track racing. In dirt track racing, motorcycles race on a flat, oval track. At some tracks the sides of the track also curve up a wall. These curves are called banks. Motorcycles ride up on the banks when they go around the turns. Professional motorcycle drivers race at speeds exceeding 100 mph.

Motocross and supercross are other types of AMA motorcycle racing. Motocross comes from the words motorcycle and cross country. These words also describe how the race is run. Just like runners who race cross country, these motorcycles race on a track that winds through countryside.

Superbike racer Rossi is on his way to victory in the 2004 Cinzano British Grand Prix.

Motocross riders race over hills and jumps on a dirt track that is constructed for the race. Riders are often in midair as they speed over steep bumps in the course. Racers also make sharp turns on the irregular track. To win, each rider must race two timed runs, called motos. The rider who completes the most laps around the course in both motos wins the race.

Supercross races usually take place on a racetrack inside a large building, like a stadium. The dirt is brought in just for race day. The hills, jumps, and turns are present only for the event. Afterward, the dirt is taken away and the stadium can be used for a different event. Supercross races have more extreme jumps and more severe turns than motocross races.

In road racing, a motorcycle's speed depends on the course. Road-racing courses are made up of public, paved roads. A supermoto race combines road racing, flat track, and motocross on one track. Try to **visualize** a track with paved roads, dirt roads, and motocross obstacles. That's supermoto. The idea behind supermoto was to determine the best all-around motorcycle racer.

Motorcycle Muscle

When it comes to proving which machine is best, the Easy Rider motorcycle holds the record. The Easy Rider looks like a rocket with two wheels. This motorcycle **variation** is called a streamliner. The Easy Rider body measures 23-feet long and, under its smooth body cover, it has two huge engines. Streamliners are built for speed.

Streamliners race a long flat track that extends for many miles. To set a speed record, motorcyclists must make two runs in a single day. Dave Campos holds the current motorcycle land-speed record. On July 19, 1990, he drove his Easy Rider motorcycle almost 323 mph. Now, that's fast!

Chapter 4
Trains on Track

As you have seen, motorcycles are made for getting people around quickly. They are definitely not practical for carrying large groups of people. Transporting lots of people from place to place requires bigger vehicles, such as trains. Trains have a long history. They did not start out as the speeding bullets we see on tracks today. Back in the 1550s, some of the roads in Germany had wooden rails. Pulling wagons by horses along wooden rails was more **efficient** than pulling wagons on dirt roads.

Two hundred years later, both the wheels and the rails were made of iron instead of wood. Horses still pulled wagons. However, the wagon wheels ran in grooves, which were narrow, cutout ruts in a road. The grooves were lined with metal.

Englishman William Jessup had an idea. He thought he could improve the wheels of the trains. Jessup tested his **hypothesis**. He made special wheels that had collars, called flanges, around each side of the rims. The flanges hung down over the edges of the rail and kept the wheel on a track. The wheels could ride on top of the tracks instead of in the grooves.

Adding Steam

Richard Trevithick, an English engineer, created the first locomotive. It had a steam engine. In 1804, Trevithick put his locomotive to the test. The locomotive hauled 10 tons of iron, 70 men, and 5 wagons. The 9-mile trip took about 2 hours.

Once steam engines were used, the creation of the modern railroad was getting closer. George Stephenson, an English inventor, built a locomotive for the mine where he worked. However, he had bigger plans. Stephenson wanted to build rail lines across England.

Riding the Rails

In 1825, George Stephenson made his own dream come true. The first rail line for passengers ran Stephenson's locomotive. It was called the Locomotion. At first it only pulled wagons of freight. People thought the steam engines were **hazardous**. So, for years the rail line continued to use horses to pull passenger wagons. It took people a while to get used to train travel, but once they did, the world caught "railroad fever." A locomotive could pull a train at 16 mph. It could also carry more freight for longer distances than horses could.

Some people **visualized** railroads as a way to get rich. Across the Atlantic, Colonel John Stevens, a U.S. inventor, realized that developing railroads would make a big difference to the way the nation did business. Stevens believed that railroads should be built across the United States. At that time, water was the fastest way to ship goods, and building canals was the way to make money. Freight entered the harbors on the East Coast and businesses shipped goods inland on the waterways. The farther inland they shipped their goods the more money they made.

All aboard! Early trains looked very different from modern ones.

Business people in the city of Baltimore, Maryland, noticed canals being built near other seaports. They were afraid that port cities near canals would take business away from Baltimore. A group of powerful Maryland citizens decided the state needed to build a railroad.

The Baltimore and Ohio Railroad (B&O) line opened for business in May 1830. At first, the B&O tried "sail cars." These railroad cars relied on sails to make them move. Then, the B&O switched to cars pulled by horses. In 1830, the railroad held a race between a locomotive called Tom Thumb and a horse. The locomotive developed engine trouble and the horse won. However, the steam locomotive soon became the favored source of railroad power.

In Charleston, South Carolina, people saw railroads as a way to bring goods farther inland. When their railroad started running in December 1830, only steam locomotives were used. These locomotives went about 20 mph. The B&O became the first railroad line to run a locomotive, but Charleston was the first to use one for passenger service.

For the next 30 years, railroad lines were built across the United States. By 1869, a person could travel by train across the entire country in days, instead of weeks or even months. That was progress! Train travel was so **overwhelmingly** fast that it became the most popular way to take a trip. Travel by other means—such as boat and wagon—**declined**.

As more rail lines were created, the trains themselves got better and better. Improvements meant fewer boiler accidents. Sleeper cars were added for long-distance travel. Trains became hotels on wheels.

For 100 years, locomotives relied on steam engines. Then, steam power was replaced. In 1925, the first diesel engines appeared in a rail yard. The internal combustion engine had made its way onto the rail line.

High-Speed Trains

With the arrival of the diesel engine, trains were able to travel at higher speeds. The diesel engine had changed the inner workings of a train. The next step was to change the outside of a train.

Train designers took some cues from airplane design. To make an airplane fly, designers had to know how air moved around a plane's body. Smoothing out edges allowed air to flow around a vehicle without **restraint**. As a result, a vehicle could move at faster speeds.

Changes made to the inside and the outside worked together. The new diesel engine didn't need a tall smoke stack, so the top and front of a train could be smoothed out. Air could move quickly around a locomotive. The new streamlined design changed the look of a train. It looked like a bullet on wheels.

The Zephyr

How fast could these new trains go? One railroad company decided to find out. On May 26, 1934, the Burlington Railroad cleared the tracks between Denver, Colorado, and Chicago, Illinois. No other train could use the rails that day. The railroad company was determined to set a speed record with its new train, the Zephyr. A train usually took about 26 hours to travel between Denver and Chicago—a distance of 1,000 miles. The train left the Denver station at dawn and began the trip to Chicago. It was going to run nonstop.

The Zephyr reached Chicago in **precisely** 13 hours and 5 minutes. The train had run from dawn to dusk without stopping. The engineers said that in some stretches the train had run at more than 112 mph! Of course, in some places its speed was slower. The train's average speed was about 77 mph. The Zephyr had made the longest nonstop run at the fastest average speed.

Bullet Trains

Thirty years later, another new train took the world by surprise. Just in time for the 1964 Olympic Games in Tokyo, Japan introduced the Shinkansen Bullet Train. The new high-speed train ran between Tokyo and Osaka at 131 mph, and this was its everyday speed, not its racing speed.

The bullet train had great speed, and it also had a new type of engine. The bullet train was powered by electricity. Wires above the tracks provided power for the train. The front car, called the power car, had wires that reached up to connect with the electric wires overhead.

The response to the bullet train was **overwhelming**. Today, there are bullet trains all across Japan. They are even used in tunnels under the ocean that connect Japan's four main islands. Bullet trains can also be found in other parts of Asia as well as in Europe, Russia, and the United States.

By the year 2000 the United States finally had a bullet train line of its own. Today, the Acela Express bullet train travels from Washington, D.C., to New York, New York, and Boston, Massachusetts. The Acela bullet train reaches speeds of up to 150 mph.

Magnetic Levitation Trains

The success of the bullet train was exciting. Japanese engineers began experimenting with a new train that used electricity and magnets for power. This new train is called a maglev train. Maglev is short for magnetic levitation. What this means is that the electricity and the magnets levitate, or raise, the train. Together they create a magnetic field and cause the train to rise into the air.

Magnets attract and repel—they pull things toward them or they push things away. The Japanese engineers use magnets to *repel* their maglev trains. On the other hand, the German engineers use magnets to *attract* their maglev trains.

Whether the magnets repel or attract, in the end, the results are the same. When the magnetic field is created, a maglev train rises above its track and moves forward. Because the train does not touch the track, there is nothing to slow it down, so maglev trains run at very high speeds. In 2003, a Japanese maglev train ran at 361 mph!

Although German and Japanese engineers test maglev trains, neither country has a maglev passenger line yet. The first maglev passenger line was built in England in the mid-1980s. The line linked two terminals at the Birmingham airport. The service was definitely not a high-speed one—its top speed was only about 10 mph. Spare parts were hard to find for the trains when they needed repairs, and so the service **declined**. The authorities decided to shut down the line and assigned the train's route to a city bus.

German engineers built a maglev train line in Shanghai, China. This maglev travels between the city and the airport. The Chinese maglev was built to transport more than 10 million passengers a year.

Chinese officials have plans to expand their maglev line. Engineers in Germany and the United States also have maglev plans in the works. Someday soon there may be a maglev line near your home.

Electric–powered bullet trains travel at speeds up to 186 mph.

Chapter 5
Taking Flight

You've seen how vehicles have sped across roads, along tracks, and even levitated above the ground. The next stage on your journey is into the sky. Have you ever dreamed of flying like a bird? Many people have shared that dream, but until fairly recently, it was an impossible wish. Trying to make wings like a bird's eventually led to the invention of the glider. In 1849, a glider carried a passenger for the first time.

Gliders fly without motors, so adding a motor to a glider was the next step. Inventors tried to fly with steam engines and gas-powered engines. Early planes with steam-powered engines carried no passengers. However, one of the early gasoline-powered engine aircrafts did have a pilot. Unfortunately, the plane did not stay in the air.

Two bicycle mechanics from Ohio were able to fly a human-operated craft. The Wright Brothers, Orville and Wilbur, made their first flight on December 17, 1903, near Kitty Hawk, North Carolina. The brothers took turns flying. During the first flight, Orville was the pilot. The plane remained in the air for just 12 seconds. The brothers tried again. On their fourth flight that day, the plane stayed in the air for 59 seconds—nearly 1 minute! The plane had flown 750 feet and had reached the then-amazing speed of 30 mph.

Early Planes

Six years after the first flight, the first yearly air show was held in France. During the show, pilots competed to see how high, how fast, and how far their planes could fly. The first planes did not look anything like today's sleek aircraft. Early planes were made of wood wrapped with canvas. Wires held the wings in place. A plane's motor had a propeller that spun around. In those early days of flight, many pilots built their own planes.

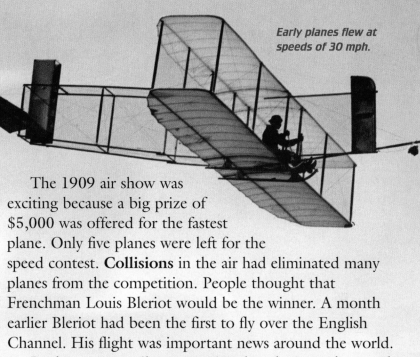

Early planes flew at speeds of 30 mph.

The 1909 air show was exciting because a big prize of $5,000 was offered for the fastest plane. Only five planes were left for the speed contest. **Collisions** in the air had eliminated many planes from the competition. People thought that Frenchman Louis Bleriot would be the winner. A month earlier Bleriot had been the first to fly over the English Channel. His flight was important news around the world.

In the contest, pilots were timed as they raced around a course one by one. American Glenn Curtiss flew first, and Bleriot flew last. To everyone's surprise, Curtiss was six seconds faster. His average speed was 46.5 mph.

Airplanes Go to Work

Airplanes were given a new role during World War I, which took place from 1914 to 1918 and involved many of the world's great powers. Planes were used to spy on the enemy. Pilots flew overhead to see where the enemy's troops were. Airplanes were also used in combat. Pilots flew behind enemy lines to drop bombs. They also fought with other planes in air battles called dogfights.

When the war was over, planes were put to work at home, too. For example, airplanes began to transport mail. The first airmail delivery in the United States took place on Long Island, New York. In 1911, Earle Ovington flew the mail from an airfield near Garden City to Mineola, a distance of less than 10 miles.

In 1918, the U.S. Post Office began regular airmail delivery. In those days, flying at night was **perceived** to be dangerous. Airmail planes only flew during the day. At night, the mail would be placed on a train. During the night, the train would make its way to a city. In the morning, the mail would be taken off the train in the city and placed on a new plane. In 1921, planes carrying airmail began flying at night. The first night flight was from San Francisco, California, to New York, New York. The plane left San Francisco before dawn on February 22 and arrived in New York near dusk on February 23. The plane's average speed was 104 mph. In the 1920s, planes also began carrying passengers. Early planes were quite small and could carry only eight passengers. Some planes were old bombers from the war with chairs installed. In 1927, the post office stopped flying airmail planes and sent the mail on passenger planes instead. The post office paid the airlines to fly the mail across the country. In fact, most cross-country mail is still sent by passenger airplanes today.

Airplanes Grow Up

Airlines wanted even bigger planes so they could carry more passengers. They wanted their planes to have more power, too. After trying several designs, the Douglas Aircraft Company made a plane that met these needs. On December 17, 1935, the DC-3 made its first flight. It was 32 years to the day after the Wright Brothers' first flight. The DC-3 had seats that could be folded down for beds. Fourteen people could sleep in luxury as they flew overnight. On daytime flights, the DC-3 could seat 21 passengers. The plane could fly at 20,000 feet, higher than ever before. It flew above the clouds at 150 to 200 mph, making the flight both smoother and shorter. Airlines all over the world bought DC-3s. Soon 90 percent of all the planes flying were DC-3s.

Jets Take Off

Imagine two people, living in different countries, who had never met having the same idea at the same time. This is how the jet engine came to be. A British Royal Air Force officer worked in England, while a German engineer worked at home in Germany. Each man produced a jet engine. They both created internal combustion engines, which meant that airplanes could fly without propellers.

As you may recall from reading about the car, an internal combustion engine needs air to work. A jet engine uses fans to suck in air. As the air **collides** with the fuel, an electric spark causes an explosion. Burning fuel shoots out of the back of the engine. As the flames of gas shoot back, they thrust the jet engine (and the plane) forward.

The German jet engine flew first. On August 27, 1939, the Heinkel He-178 became the first jet-powered flight in history. A week later, World War II began. Countries needed to use planes for combat. The German air force became the first to use the jet engine in a fighter plane. The first jet fighter had two engines, and could fly 540 mph!

After the war, airline companies began to fly planes with jet engines. The British Overseas Airways Corporation (BOAC) was the first. In 1952, BOAC began flying the Comet 1. This jet-powered plane carried 36 passengers at a speed of 450 mph.

A year later, three Comets broke apart in midair, killing everyone onboard the flights. Experts ran tests. The tests showed that the metal around the Comets' square windows had grown weak. After takeoff, this weakness caused the planes to break apart. Safety **precautions** were needed. BOAC stopped flying Comets until the plane was redesigned.

Look up! A trail of vapor follows the jet plane.

Five years later, the Comet made a comeback. The newer, safer Comet had smaller, round windows. The windows' new size and shape allowed the metal around them to better withstand air pressure at high altitudes. In 1958, however, the Comet wasn't the only passenger jet people could fly. The Boeing 707 had arrived.

Pan American World Airways, nicknamed Pan Am, flew the Boeing 707. Pan Am flew passengers from the United States to countries overseas. In 1958, Pan Am began jet service with a flight from New York, New York, to Paris, France. The jet flew 600 mph at **precisely** 32,000 feet. It flew faster than the Comet and higher than the DC-3. There were 111 passengers on board that New York-to-Paris Boeing 707 flight.

Early overseas flights from New York included a stop in Canada to refuel. It was not long before airlines realized that they needed planes that did not have to stop to refuel. After Boeing made changes to the 707, Pan Am flew nonstop from New York to London.

The response to the new 707 was **overwhelming**. Airlines everywhere bought jets. Jets flew faster, higher, and farther. They could also carry more passengers, which meant they made more money for an airline. What was the next challenge? The next step was to carry passengers at speeds that exceeded the speed of sound.

At 600 mph, the Boeing 707 ushered in the jet age.

The Supersonic Age

Supersonic means "faster than the speed of sound." Sound travels through air at about 760 mph at sea level. In the early days of flight, flying faster than the speed of sound was thought to be impossible. Nobody knew whether a pilot could control a plane at such a high speed. However, shortly after World War II, this amazing feat took place in an X-plane, an experimental plane that was built at the request of the U.S. government. On October 14, 1947, test pilot Chuck Yeager flew faster than the speed of sound. Although the speed of sound at sea level is about 760 mph, at higher altitudes, sound travels at different speeds. Yeager flew 700 mph at an altitude of 43,000 feet, faster than the speed of sound. A noise like thunder, called a sonic boom, resulted. It was caused by pressure changes due to fast speed.

In 1964, the U.S. Congress set aside money for an SST, a supersonic transport. However, enthusiasm for the project **declined**. People did not want to hear a sonic boom when a plane landed. They were also worried about air pollution. Work on the project came to a halt.

French and British scientists worked together to make an SST called the Concorde. The Concorde took off at 250 mph and rapidly reached 1,350 mph, flying at twice the speed of sound. A Concorde flight from New York to London took 3 hours and 20 minutes. That same flight took 7 hours on a Boeing 747. A ticket to fly from New York to London at **maximum** speed sold for $12,000 to $16,000. In 2003, the Concorde made its last flight. Not enough people could afford to fly on the supersonic transport. What's next for fast-flying vehicles? Engineers are trying to build high-speed transport planes. These planes will outstrip the Concorde's speed and carry 300 passengers. Perhaps one day in the future you will have the chance to fly in one of these speedy giants.

Chapter 6
Soaring Into Outer Space

The fastest vehicles on the planet travel in space. When you orbit Earth, you travel at the amazing speed of 17,000 mph. This was true when astronaut John Glenn became the first U.S. astronaut to orbit Earth in 1962, and it is still true today.

Rockets are the vehicles that take humans into space. In thirteenth-century China, the first rockets were bamboo tubes with gunpowder placed inside and shot into the sky. For hundreds of years, rockets **functioned** as fireworks or weapons. It wasn't until the twentieth century that rockets powered vehicles.

U.S. inventor Robert Goddard was the first to try liquid fuel in a rocket. In 1926, he used liquid oxygen and gasoline to power a rocket. The 10-foot rocket shot into the sky at 60 mph. It climbed 41 feet before it turned over and crashed into a cabbage field. Amazingly, all of this happened in two-and-a-half seconds!

Goddard **hypothesized** that a rocket could reach the moon. When others heard about his ideas, they made fun of him. The newspaper *The New York Times* wrote about Goddard, saying that he didn't understand science. Goddard continued his work anyway. He built bigger rockets that flew faster and higher.

During World War II, German leadership welcomed Goddard's ideas. The German government made the V-2 rocket. The V-2 was used to bomb cities during the war. The head of the German rocket team was Wernher von Braun. He wanted to place **restraints** on the use of rockets. Wernher von Braun did not want to bomb cities. His **ambition** was to send rockets to the Moon. After the war, von Braun and his team came to the United States to build rockets. In 1958, one of their rockets sent a satellite into space. The U.S. space program had begun.

Roaring Into Space

Six months after the first U.S. satellite was sent into space, the government formed the National Aeronautics and Space Administration (NASA) to be in charge of space exploration. The Soviet Union (which included Russia and other countries near it at that time) had already sent their first satellite into space. The United States wanted to compete. The race into space was on!

Rockets were the key to taking humans into outer space. The two countries competed to build more and more powerful rockets. Scientists sent those rockets into space as they tested new ideas.

In 1957, the Soviets sent a dog into outer space. The United States sent a chimpanzee in January 1961. Three months later, Russian astronaut Yuri Gagarin was the first human in space. He orbited Earth for 108 minutes.

Reaching the Moon was the next challenge. A new series of rockets was built, and named for the planet Saturn. In July 1969, a Saturn rocket launched the *Apollo 11* mission. Two U.S. astronauts, Neil Armstrong and Buzz Aldrin, were the first humans to land on the Moon.

Blast off! A rocket is launched to the moon.

After reaching the Moon, the next step was to live and work in space. Skylab was America's first space station. Saturn rockets played two roles in the mission. The Skylab workshop was made from a section of a Saturn rocket. Another Saturn rocket launched Skylab into space.

Three different crews of astronauts lived and worked in Skylab in 1973 and 1974. Each crew stayed in space a little longer than the one before. Scientists wanted to see how space travel affected the human body. The crews did research while orbiting Earth. The research was designed to reveal what kinds of **restraints** were placed on the body because of the conditions in space.

The Space Shuttle was NASA's next big project. Early rockets could be used only once. After a mission, they became space junk. Creating a reusable rocket made a huge difference in what was possible to achieve in space. The reusable Space Shuttle has three main parts: the external fuel tank, the booster rockets, and the orbiter. Only the orbiter goes into space.

Two minutes after liftoff, the work of the two booster rockets is done. The rockets have taken the astronauts from 0 to 3,438 mph. Then, the two rockets separate from the shuttle and fall into the ocean. Later, the rockets are picked up and used again for the next launch.

The big external fuel tank still has work to do. In the next 6.5 minutes, it carries the astronauts 200 miles above Earth's surface, traveling at 17,000 mph. When the fuel tank is empty, the shuttle lets go of it. The fuel tank breaks up as it falls through space so nothing is left to fall on Earth.

The Space Shuttle orbiter is like a plane. It has wings, and it lands on a runway. The shuttle's runway is much longer than an airport runway because the shuttle lands at 300 mph. To help it slow down, the shuttle has a parachute just like a drag racer does.

The International Space Station

Rockets made the space program possible. In 1969, rockets made it possible for men to reach the Moon and even walk on it. Today, rockets take men and women into space to build the International Space Station.

Astronauts on the space station stay in space much longer than earlier astronauts. John Glenn was in space for 4 hours and 55 minutes. The last astronauts on the Moon were in space for 12 days, 13 hours, and 52 minutes. Today, astronauts work on the space station for 6 months at a time.

The astronauts on the space station experience zero-gravity. They "float" in space because their bodies are moving at the same speed as the space station itself. That is, they are orbiting Earth at 17,000 mph. Staying in space so long affects how the human body **functions**. Human bones and muscles slowly break down in zero gravity. As part of their daily routine, astronauts in space exercise 2 hours a day.

Astronaut Training

Do you think you might want to become an astronaut? Here's what it takes. First, to be chosen for astronaut training, a candidate must meet certain requirements of education. Once chosen, astronauts train long and hard to get ready for space. Basic training lasts a year, and takes place on land, underwater, and in the air. Future astronauts attend classes to learn about traveling in space. They also have survival training. For example, they have to tread water for 10 minutes without stopping. They must swim laps in a pool with a flight suit and shoes on. Scuba diving is also part of astronaut school, including wearing scuba gear and working on equipment under the water.

In order to get an idea of what living in space feels like, astronauts train in a cargo plane. The plane flies continuously up and down so passengers can experience weightlessness. This plane has been called the Vomit Comet. Can you imagine the reason for the jet's nickname? It comes from the airsickness many experience on these flights.

Astronaut candidates enjoying zero-gravity training.

Astronauts fly planes as part of their training. Pilots also fly a total of 100 hours in a shuttle training craft, a jet that handles like the orbiter. Learning about the orbiter is done step-by-step. First, astronauts learn about how each system in the orbiter works. After their systems training, astronauts begin training in a simulator. A simulator is just like the shuttle—only it's on the ground, not in the sky. Software programs make astronauts feel as if they are actually flying. To train for a flight, astronauts train in the simulators for 300 hours.

Learning how to live in space is also part of an astronaut's training. Astronauts must learn how to prepare meals, stow equipment, and throw away trash. Because items are weightless in space, every item has a place. If items are not attached to something, they will float around. Even the astronauts will float! Using straps while they sleep **enables** astronauts to sleep without floating. They put their sleeping bag in the pilot's seat and strap themselves in. They can also attach a sleeping bag to a wall and sleep there.

Until now, the U.S. government has been in charge of going into space. Citizens' taxes paid for the space programs. The government made all of the decisions about space travel. A special contest may change all that.

The Ansari X Prize

What is the Ansari X Prize? Named for the Ansari family, one of its biggest supporters, the X Prize offered a $10 million award for space travel. To win the X Prize, a team had to send a rocket ship 62.5 miles high before the end of 2004. The craft had to carry at least three people into space two times during a two-week period. What was the reason behind the X Prize? It was all about space tourism. The founder's **ambition** is to carry tourists into space. That is why the competition stated that the craft had to carry passengers. According to the contest rules, each team could not get any help from its government. After the prize was announced in 1996, more than 20 teams from seven countries registered to compete for the prize.

On October 4, 2004, test pilot Mike Melville flew *SpaceShipOne* 62.5 miles into space for the second time in a two-week period. He became the first person to fly a private craft into space and won the X Prize. Melville's ship was dropped from the belly of another plane before he rocketed up into space. Once there, he was weightless for three minutes. Then, he came back to Earth and landed. More flights are planned, and teams are at work around the globe. Private travel into space may be just around the corner. Can you **visualize** yourself flying through space at 17,000 mph? It is entirely possible that you will have this opportunity in your lifetime. After all, imagination and hard work have led to many dreams becoming realities. Perhaps your dream will speed you far into the future.

Mike Melville's craft uses rubber and laughing gas to power its rocket!

Mind-Boggling BRIDGES

by Ellen Dreyer

CHAPTER 1

Super Spans

Imagine you are looking up at an enormous steel and concrete bridge. The bridge rises more than 500 feet overhead. That's about as tall as a 40-story building! Massive cables run from the bridge towers to a roadway that hangs over racing water. Vehicles speed across the roadway's span of 6,500 feet. You listen to their thunderous rumble. You shake your head in wonder. How does this bridge bear the weight of so many cars and trucks? How does it span a distance of more than one mile without collapsing?

Bridges have played an important role in human history. When a stream, river, or ravine blocks a traveler's way, a bridge allows the traveler to pass over it. Bridges have existed for as long as people have had the need to travel. Not much is known about bridges in prehistoric times though. It is likely that prehistoric people used bridges provided by nature, such as fallen tree trunks or stepping-stones. As centuries passed, people began to **design** and build bridges. They used natural materials, such as wood, stone, and vines. They also used their strength, intelligence, **ingenuity**, and courage.

Some early human-made bridges were as simple as a single rope stretched across a river. People would grasp the rope with their hands and legs and pull themselves across. This method worked well for one person at a time, but what if someone wanted to bring a wagon across the bridge? Obviously, a single rope wouldn't work!

Over time, bridge builders used different materials so that bridges could bear larger and heavier loads. In Asia, South America, and other parts of the world, people made rope walkways by knotting many ropes together. Starting around 1200 BCE, bridge builders began to use iron. More recently, bridge builders turned to steel. Steel is a **durable** metal made from iron and other materials.

In this book, you'll learn about a bridge that was built about 2,000 years ago but is still being used today, a bridge that was moved from a river in England to a desert in the United States, and some bridges that have fallen down. You'll also learn about three kinds of bridges: arch, suspension, and cable-stayed.

Arch bridges use a half-circle as their basic shape. They are very strong, as the ancient Romans proved. Arch bridges built by the ancient Romans have lasted for centuries.

This tower of the Golden Gate Bridge in San Francisco, California, is so high that it can make you dizzy just looking up at it!

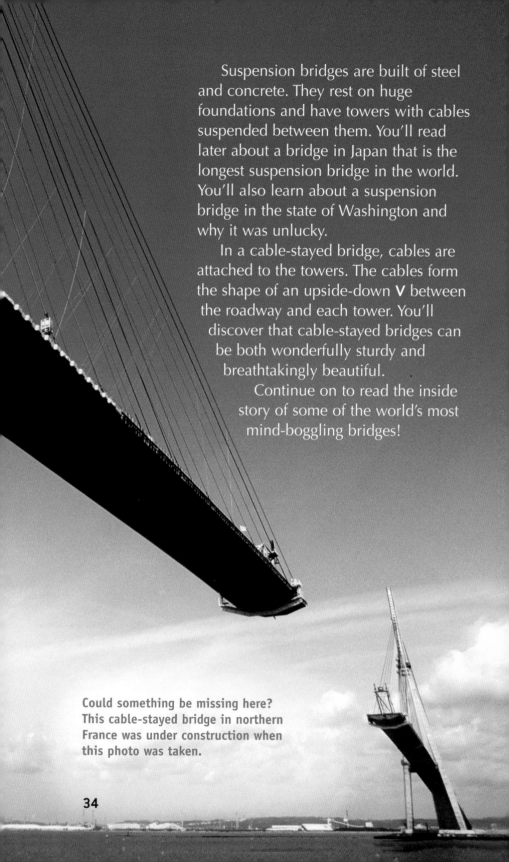

Suspension bridges are built of steel and concrete. They rest on huge foundations and have towers with cables suspended between them. You'll read later about a bridge in Japan that is the longest suspension bridge in the world. You'll also learn about a suspension bridge in the state of Washington and why it was unlucky.

In a cable-stayed bridge, cables are attached to the towers. The cables form the shape of an upside-down **V** between the roadway and each tower. You'll discover that cable-stayed bridges can be both wonderfully sturdy and breathtakingly beautiful.

Continue on to read the inside story of some of the world's most mind-boggling bridges!

Could something be missing here? This cable-stayed bridge in northern France was under construction when this photo was taken.

CHAPTER 2

A Roman Wonder

Picture yourself in southern Gaul, a part of the vast Roman Empire that is in present-day France. The year is 100 CE. A great aqueduct, or channel for transporting water, has just been built. The aqueduct brings water 31 miles from springs near the Roman town of Ucetia (present-day Uzes) to the city of Nemausus (present-day Nîmes). The most amazing part of the aqueduct is a stone bridge with three levels that each contain arches. The bridge is about 160 feet high and 900 feet long. It towers above the Gardon River valley. Today, this bridge is known as the Pont du Gard. (In French, the word *pont* means "bridge.") It is over 2,000 years old.

Fresh, clean water was very important to the Romans. They built aqueducts all over the empire to carry water from one place to another. The aqueduct that includes the Pont du Gard carried an **abundant** supply of fresh water to the 50,000 citizens of Nemausus. It provided about 100 gallons per day for each person!

The Romans made a huge **contribution** to architecture and engineering. They built aqueducts and other structures to exact **specifications**. Roman aqueducts were raised off the ground. They were covered to protect the water from sunlight and falling objects that could contaminate it.

The Romans didn't have machines to pump water through their aqueducts. They didn't know how to use electricity. They relied on their intelligence and the powerful forces **concealed** in nature. Gravity was the main natural force behind the success of Roman aqueducts.

How strong is the Pont du Gard? A devastating earthquake in 1448 didn't shake it. The frequent flooding of the powerful Gardon River has not destroyed it. Wars and various periods of rebuilding have not caused its collapse.

The bottom level has been a walkway for hundreds of years. Pillars on one side of this walkway were made narrower in the 1500s so that pack mules could use the walkway. The walkway was widened again in the late 1700s for wheeled vehicles. These changes damaged the limestone. Deep ruts were created when wheels passed over it. After years of misuse, the Pont du Gard was in a state of **decay** and dangerously weakened. Finally, in the mid-1800s, Napoleon III of France ordered the bridge to be restored. The ancient bridge was saved from collapse. Today, more than 1 million people from all over the world visit the Pont du Gard each year.

The nearly 2,000-year-old Pont du Gard is a major tourist attraction today.

The Mighty Arch

The Romans were engineering wizards. They **designed** impressive and enduring structures. Caius Julius Lacer, a Roman engineer, was buried near a bridge he built. The words, "I leave a bridge forever in the centuries of the world," were written on his tombstone. He might as well have been talking about the Pont du Gard.

The arch is a key factor behind the strength of the Pont du Gard. The Romans didn't invent the arch, but they did improve on its **design**. The Roman arch is able to bear incredible amounts of weight. It is made from wedge-shaped stones or bricks arranged in a semi-circle. A special stone called the keystone sits at the very top of the arch. The keystone directs the pressure of the stones out along the arch, toward the ground. This sharing of weight helps to make the arch an extremely strong and stable structure. It sounds simple, doesn't it? Consider this. The arches built by the Romans were held together only by the weight of the stones pressing against each other. The stones had to be cut by hand and fit together perfectly in order for the arches to stand.

How do arch bridges work? The weight of an arch bridge is distributed along the curve of the arch, instead of pressing straight down into the ground. Supports at either end of the arch bridge, called abutments, carry the thrust of the load. They also prevent the ends of the bridge from spreading out and causing the bridge to cave in.

The builders of the Pont du Gard faced many building challenges. They had to contend with the shifting, muddy river bottom in order to sink the bridge foundations. They also had to contend with the Gardon River. It is fast-flowing and floods from time to time. The river must have been a nightmare for the teams of men (probably slaves) who worked on the Pont du Gard's foundations.

Bridge With Roman Arches

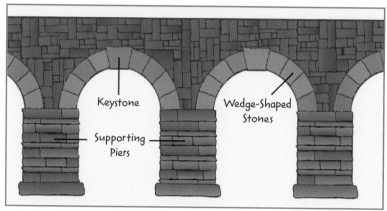

The ancient Romans used the semicircular arch to build many bridges and buildings.

How did the Romans build the bridge's piers, or supports, in the riverbed? First, they built a water-tight space called a cofferdam. To build a cofferdam, the Romans placed a wide circle of tight-fitting timber poles around the place where they planned to build each pier. Then, they built a second circle of tight-fitting poles inside the first circle. Workers dumped a large amount of clay between the two circles. Then, the workers bailed water out of the inner circle where they would build the pier. The Romans also discovered a way to tame the strong current in the river. They made the piers pointy at both sides to reduce the force of the water passing under the bridge.

After the piers were sunk, workers put up temporary timber frames called falseworks. They laid the stones for each arch along the **contours** of a falsework. This temporary falsework helped the builders make certain that the stones fit together perfectly. The Pont du Gard was the tallest aqueduct ever built by the Romans. The bridge's engineers determined that they needed to build three separate levels of arches in order to make the bridge as high as they wanted it to be.

On the bottom level of the Pont du Gard, there are 6 arches. These arches are the widest in the bridge. Their lengths range from 51 to 80 feet across. The second level contains 11 arches that are all the same size. The third, or topmost, level has 35 narrower arches. The third level contains the water channel itself. It is the only level in which mortar was used to hold the stones together.

The 31-mile water channel that carries water to and from the Pont du Gard is another amazing engineering feature. The aqueduct's engineers needed to make sure that water would flow well through the channel. The springs at Ucetia were the source of the water. These springs were only 55 feet higher than the city of Nemausus, the water's destination. The engineers discovered that the slope or incline of the channel could be no steeper than about 20 inches per mile. A slope this slight cannot be seen by the naked eye. In fact, the channel looks perfectly flat!

How did Roman engineers figure out just how steep the water channel needed to be? They probably looked to nature for answers. A mountain stream flows faster where the slope of the mountain is steeper. Even parts of a streambed that appear to be flat **conceal** a slight slope that allows the water to keep flowing.

The engineers had to make precise calculations so that the water would flow properly. What calculation tools did they have to work with? The engineers had a wax tablet for writing notes and an abacus, or beaded counting frame. They also had a special instrument called a level. The Romans used the level to find out if a line or surface was horizontal. With these simple tools, the Romans constructed a **monumental** structure that you can still admire today.

This lead pipe from a Roman aqueduct is about 2,000 years old.

CHAPTER 3

London Bridges Through the Ages

London Bridge is falling down,
falling down, falling down;
London Bridge is falling down,
My fair lady!

Do you recognize this famous nursery rhyme? Do you realize that the London Bridge has actually been rebuilt many times throughout history? In fact, one London Bridge really did fall down!

The incredible and often violent story of the London Bridge began with the ancient Romans. Historians think the Romans built a timber bridge over the Thames River sometime after they invaded Britain in 43 CE. The Romans founded the city of Londinium near this bridge. It is likely that the bridge fell into **decay** in the fifth century, at the same time that Londinium did.

Between the fifth century and the thirteenth century, a series of timber bridges were built near the former site of the Roman bridge. No one knows exactly how many timber bridges were built or how each bridge was destroyed. The next London Bridge on record was built in the tenth century. In around the year 984, a widow was accused of putting pins in the image of a man she didn't like. She was sentenced to an awful death. She was tied to the bridge and drowned when the tide rose.

Another timber bridge was built in 993, just before Danish warriors invaded Britain. The Danes sailed up the Thames to attack London. London's citizens gathered on the bridge and successfully fought them off. In 1014, a Danish king named Olaf attacked London. He commanded his warriors to attach ropes from their boats to the bridge and then row away. The warriors managed to row so hard that the bridge fell down!

After Olaf's invasion, several more timber bridges were built. Each one was destroyed by fire or swept away by the river. Near the end of the twelfth century, a man named Peter de Colechurch decided to **design** a permanent arch bridge over the Thames River. This London Bridge took 33 years to build, but the stone bridge lasted for 600 years!

Building this bridge was a dangerous and complicated task. Ocean tides caused water levels in the Thames River to vary greatly. Also, the river's swift current may have become stronger after some of the piers were built. The piers forced the river to pass through narrower openings.

Do you remember how the Romans built the piers for the Pont du Gard? Workers used the same method to build the piers for Peter de Colechurch's bridge. They sank two circles of timber poles into the river bottom. One circle was inside the other. Workers filled the inner circle with rocks and hammered planks on top of the rocks. Then, they laid masonry for the piers on top of the planks.

upper left:
The London Bridge in the seventeenth century
lower right:
The London Bridge in 1831. What differences can you see in these two images of the bridge?

41

Peter de Colechurch probably didn't have an exact or overall plan for the new London Bridge. Construction progressed as weather and available money allowed. This lack of planning did not produce a graceful bridge. The completed bridge had an **abundance** of arches. These arches had different widths and **contours**. They were strung across the river like a necklace of mismatched beads.

The passageways between the piers of the bridge were very narrow. The river water created dangerous rapids as it rushed through the piers at the start of high and low tides. Would you have been willing to take a boat through one of these passageways when the rapids were at their strongest? Steering a boat between the piers at these times was called "shooting the bridge." It wasn't for the timid! Many people drowned when their boats capsized.

Over time, houses and shops were built on top of the bridge, on both sides of the roadway. People could buy tobacco, cloth, pins, needles, food, drink, and other **necessities** from shops and taverns. Starting in 1281, bridge wardens on one side of the bridge collected tolls. People on foot, on horseback, in wheeled vehicles, and leading livestock were all charged. Boats were also charged for passing under the bridge.

Starting in 1304, the tower gates of the bridge served a very gruesome purpose. The **decaying** heads and limbs of traitors and criminals were stuck on the gates, one of which became known as Traitor's Gate. This terrible tradition continued until 1678.

Who do you think the "my fair lady" was of the nursery rhyme? Many people think it was Eleanor of Aquitaine, the wife of King Henry II. Londoners didn't actually think her "fair" at all. They hated her for spending tolls from the bridge on herself instead of on much-needed repairs. After all, some sections of the bridge really were in danger of falling down!

Moving a Giant

In the middle of the eighteenth century, an engineer named Labelye was hired to renovate the old and decaying London Bridge. He removed the ancient buildings on top of the bridge and widened the roadway. To make the waterway wider, he removed the bridge's central pier and replaced two arches with one wide, central arch. These changes had an unintended result. The bridge became unstable because the force of the river was focused on the center arch. By the early 1800s, London Bridge was in danger of falling down...again!

It was clear that rebuilding the bridge was a **necessity**. Several engineers **contributed** plans for a new bridge. John Rennie, a Scottish engineer, was chosen for the job. His new London Bridge opened in 1831. It was built of granite and had semicircular Roman arches that supported the weight of the roadway on top.

Rennie's London Bridge was heavily used by pedestrians, wagons, and, eventually, automobiles until the **decade** of the 1960s. At that time, engineers discovered it was sinking into the clay at the bottom of the Thames River. The bridge simply wasn't built to handle the volume of traffic passing over it for so many **decades**.

Plans were made to build a new bridge, but city officials did not want to destroy Rennie's historic bridge. They finally decided to put it up for auction. The highest bidder would become the bridge's new owner.

A wealthy American named Robert McCulloch was the successful bidder. In 1968, he paid almost $2.5 million for the bridge. That was the highest price ever paid for an antique up to that point. Some say that McCulloch was under the mistaken impression that he'd bought the Tower Bridge, another famous bridge in London. Others say that he knew exactly which bridge he had purchased.

The nineteenth-century London Bridge seems right at home in Lake Havasu City, Arizona.

Once McCulloch owned the London Bridge, he faced a major decision. Where should he put the bridge? McCulloch's answer to this question was unusual, to say the least. He decided to move it to the Arizona desert!

In 1963, McCulloch founded a leisure and retirement community in Arizona called Lake Havasu City. In 1968, it was still a small town. McCulloch thought that the London Bridge would attract people to his community and contribute to the city's growth.

Rebuilding the bridge in Arizona meant that first it had to be taken apart stone by stone. An **ingenious** system was developed for keeping track of where every stone belonged in the bridge. Each stone was marked with four numbers that indicated its position. The first number told which span the stone came from. The second number told which row of stones it was from. The last two numbers told how the stone was positioned in the row.

Workers responsible for this numbering chore discovered that there were already old code numbers on the stones. These original numbers were probably written on the rocks before they left the quarries. Rennie's workers probably used the numbers to determine where to place the stones in his bridge.

Not all the stones from the London Bridge made it to Lake Havasu City. McCulloch owed taxes to the city of London. To pay his debt, he gave some of the bridge stones back to the city. The city auctioned off the stones for cash.

If you bought an enormous stone bridge, how would you move it to its new location? The stones traveled 10,000 miles, from London to Long Beach, California, by ship. From Long Beach, they were trucked to Lake Havasu City. A special human-made water channel was created so that water would run under the bridge. The Lord Mayor of London traveled to Lake Havasu City and laid the cornerstone of the bridge on September 23, 1968. The bridge's reconstruction began. The bridge was completed three years later, at a cost of $7 million.

Many people laughed when McCulloch purchased the London Bridge. It seems that he had the last laugh though. Since the bridge's arrival in Lake Havasu City, the city has grown considerably. The area and its notable bridge attract an **abundance** of visitors each year.

What did Londoners do without Rennie's London Bridge? In 1973, a new, modern bridge was constructed at the site of the old one. It handles a lot of traffic over the Thames, including an occasional flock of sheep. Ancient custom permits every Londoner to drive sheep across the bridge. Perhaps this old tradition reminds Londoners of the many London bridges that have stood on the same site since the history of their city began.

CHAPTER 4

Spectacular Disasters

On the morning of November 7, 1940, a windstorm in Puget Sound near Tacoma, Washington, whipped waves into a frenzy. The waters of the sound weren't the only things that were riled up, however. The four-month-old Tacoma Narrows Bridge was swaying more vigorously than usual. The bridge was a slender, two-lane suspension bridge that linked mainland Washington with the Olympic Peninsula.

Thrill-seekers drove hundreds of miles just to experience a rolling ride across Galloping Gertie.

People knew that the Tacoma Narrows Bridge rolled on windy days. In fact, the bridge had been given the nickname "Galloping Gertie." People driving on it often felt as if they were riding a roller coaster! They would notice a car in front of them dipping down and disappearing from sight on a bridge that was supposed to be straight and flat. The bridge's wave-like movements frightened some drivers and made others seasick. Nevertheless, people continued to use the bridge.

As that November morning wore on, the wind speed rose to 42 miles per hour. The bridge's motions became more violent. The roadway twisted back and forth. One side rose 28 feet higher than the other, while the roadway's surface rolled in continuous waves.

Engineers were called in to observe these strange motions. An engineer named Clark Eldridge described the movements in a report. He wrote, "...The entire main span appeared to be twisting about a neutral point at the center of the span in somewhat the manner of a corkscrew." He called the weather bureau and learned that the wind would probably die down later that day. The wind didn't die down in time to save the bridge, however.

At about 11:00 a.m., Galloping Gertie began to tear apart. First, the wind ripped some of her suspender cables off. Then, a 600-foot section of the main span plunged into the water. The rest of the main span continued to twist violently. Finally, the bridge snapped in two and collapsed completely.

Fortunately, there were no human deaths, but there was one dog that perished. A newspaper editor named Leonard Coatsworth had driven his car onto the bridge. His dog Tubby was inside. Tubby was too frightened to leave the car, so his owner had to flee without him. Here is part of Coatsworth's account:

"On hands and knees most of the time, I crawled 500 yards or more to the towers…My breath was coming in gasps; my knees were raw and bleeding, my hands bruised and swollen from gripping the concrete curb…Toward the last, I risked rising to my feet and running a few yards at a time…Safely back at the toll plaza, I saw the bridge in its final collapse and saw my car plunge into the Narrows."

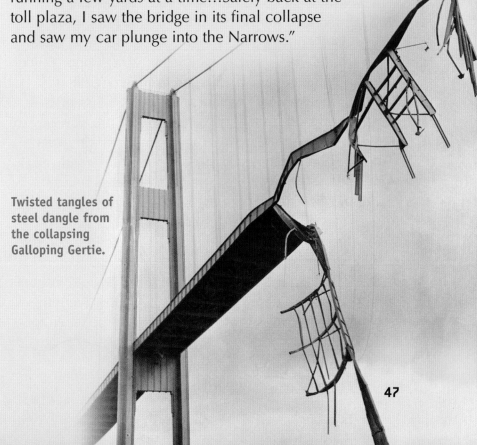

Twisted tangles of steel dangle from the collapsing Galloping Gertie.

Urgent Questions

The collapse of Galloping Gertie was one of the most **monumental** bridge disasters in history. Many eyewitnesses were at the scene, including several engineers. What happened when the bridge collapsed was clear. What wasn't clear was why the bridge failed.

Gertie's designer, Leon S. Moisseiff, was a recognized authority on long-span suspension bridges. His plan for the Tacoma Narrows Bridge was considered **ingenious**. Was this respected authority responsible for erecting a spectacular failure?

One of Moisseiff's objectives was to build a bridge with graceful **contours**. Gertie stretched 7,392 feet across the Tacoma Narrows but was also only 39 feet wide. These measurements made the bridge the narrowest long-span suspension bridge ever built. Did the bridge collapse because it was too narrow or too long?

Over the years, suspension bridges had become gradually longer, narrower, and more flexible. In the past, trusses had supported the weight of a bridge and loads going over it. These triangular-shaped steel supports were large and unattractive. As a result, bridge engineers **designed** new bridges with smaller and smaller trusses.

In the **decade** of the 1930s, engineers found a way to eliminate trusses altogether. They developed the plate girder, a solid metal beam that supported the roadway from underneath. Moisseiff used plate girders on Galloping Gertie. Was the use of plate girders instead of trusses a fatal flaw in the **design** of the bridge?

Gertie had passed wind-tunnel tests to determine the effects of wind on the bridge's stability. Bridge experts had concluded that even gale-force winds would not be strong enough to cause the bridge's collapse. Were the tests inaccurate? Were errors in the tests responsible for Gertie's failure?

Vital Answers

A board was set up to investigate the reasons for Galloping Gertie's collapse. The board reported that the wind caused the bridge "to swing back and forth with a steady rhythm." One investigator stated that the bridge actually "shook itself to death."

Why did Gertie shake so violently in the wind? Part of the answer is that the bridge was too flexible. The great length, narrow width, and shallow depth of the bridge made it overly responsive to wind. Another part of the answer is that the plate girders did not brace the bridge **sufficiently**. The girders did not absorb the force of the wind. The girders also blocked the wind instead of letting it pass through the bridge.

The wind did not actually knock down the bridge. Instead, the wind caused the bridge to vibrate so much that it eventually tore itself apart. The reasons for the bridge's collapse made one thing perfectly clear. Engineers needed to rethink the way that suspension bridges were **designed**.

Until the **decade** of the 1940s, the study of how wind affects objects was more or less limited to airplanes. Engineers did not completely understand how wind affects other objects, including bridges. The tests that engineers used to determine wind resistance were **incomplete** by today's standards.

Moisseiff took full responsibility for Galloping Gertie's collapse, but the disaster wasn't his fault. The problem lay in the limits of scientific understanding at the time. Bridge engineers realized that their knowledge was **incomplete**. They went back to the drawing board. Their goal was to discover what went wrong and how to avoid the same problems in the future.

A New Beginning

A four-year research program was started after Gertie's collapse. It was the first research program to result from a bridge failure. Researchers at the University of Washington built an **ingenious** new wind tunnel. They also built the first three-dimensional bridge models with the same properties as actual bridges.

How did the researchers use the wind tunnel and the bridge models? They used the wind tunnel to test how models of a new Tacoma Narrows Bridge would react to various wind conditions. They used these to predict how the actual bridge would react to wind. They also tested the stability of the bridge. One result was that engineers used triangular trusses in the new suspension bridge to make it more stable.

The new Tacoma Narrows Bridge was soon under construction. Engineers applied their greater understanding to build a more stable bridge. They made the new bridge both safe and beautiful. In the end, Gertie's collapse **contributed** greatly to the science of bridge building. Parts of the old bridge still lie on the bottom of Puget Sound. They are a reminder of how **incomplete** understanding of bridge design was in 1940 and how far it has advanced since then.

Can you find the triangular trusses below the span of the new Tacoma Narrows Bridge?

Multiple Disasters

Gertie's collapse wasn't the only major bridge disaster in history. One infamous bridge disaster occurred on December 28, 1879, in Queensferry, Scotland. During a violent thunderstorm, a passenger train rumbled onto the Tay Bridge that crossed the Firth (Bay) of Tay. Just then, the bridge buckled and collapsed. More than 70 passengers fell to a watery death below. Investigators never identified the main cause of the disaster.

On January 10, 1889, disaster struck the Falls View Suspension Bridge that connected New York State and Canada near Niagara Falls. A terrible storm raged the night before the disaster. Ferocious winds broke a fastening on the bridge. Finally, the bridge tore away and fell into the gorge below.

One of the worst bridge disasters on record occurred in fairly recent times. On May 9, 1980, a blinding thunderstorm hit Tampa Bay, Florida. A freight ship called the Summit Venture plowed into the 4-mile-long Sunshine Skyway Bridge. The ship's crew did not see the bridge because it was **concealed** by rain. A long section of the bridge plunged into the bay. Thirty-five people in cars and a bus fell from the bridge to their deaths.

Taming Destructive Forces

Today, engineers know a great deal about forces that destroy bridges. They can add trusses to bridges to brace them against the force of wind. They can also use dampeners to reduce destructive vibrations caused by wind. Dampeners are devices that keep vibrations from shaking a bridge apart.

Weather is one force that engineers cannot control. Engineers are able, however, to lessen the effects of weather. They accomplish this by using the best materials and bridge-building **specifications** presently known.

CHAPTER 5

Sunshine Bridge
for the Sunshine State

A new Sunshine Skyway Bridge was built to replace the one that was damaged in 1980. Is this new Sunshine Skyway more than a bridge? Is it an **ingenious** work of art? Many people would say yes. The beautiful Sunshine Skyway links St. Petersburg and Bradenton, Florida. It is the world's longest concrete cable-stayed bridge. It has an overall length of 5.5 miles. Its cables are made of steel.

The first **phase** of construction on the new Sunshine Skyway began just days after the first Sunshine Skyway was damaged. The new bridge was open to traffic seven years later, in 1987. It has won many engineering and **design** awards, including the Presidential Design Award from the National Endowment of the Arts.

Most cable-stayed bridges in the United States have been built in the last few **decades**. The designs of cable-stayed bridges and suspension bridges are similar. Both types of bridges have towers and cables. The two types of bridges support their roadways differently, however. In a suspension bridge, the cables ride across the top of the towers. The weight of the roadway is transferred to massive supports called anchorages at either end of the bridge. In a cable-stayed bridge, the towers support the complete weight of the roadway.

The new Sunshine Skyway was one of the first cable-stayed bridges to have cables attached to the center of the roadway, instead of the outside. The bridge's **intricate** web of cables does not block the view of Tampa Bay. The pipes that surround the Skyway's cables are painted bright yellow. The yellow cables represent Florida, the "Sunshine State."

Safety First

The engineers who **designed** the new Sunshine Skyway Bridge learned from the fate of the old bridge. They were very aware of the **necessity** of building a safer bridge. They were particularly concerned about protecting the piers of the bridge from ships.

To protect the piers, the engineers equipped the new bridge with 36 "dolphins." The dolphins are big, concrete bumpers built around the bridge's piers. The dolphins are incredibly strong. Each one can withstand being struck by a ship that weighs 87,000 tons! Clearance under the bridge is a **monumental** 190 feet. This height allows even the tallest ships to pass underneath.

The deck of the bridge is made from **durable** concrete. A network of reinforced wire cables is **concealed** inside the concrete. These materials form a rigid structure that supports the roadway. The strong roadway is needed for the 20,000 cars that cross the bridge each day.

"Dolphins" protect the piers of the new Sunshine Skyway Bridge in Florida.

A Smart Choice

Cable-stayed bridges became popular with bridge builders after World War II. Steel was in short supply at that time. Cable-stayed bridges require less steel than suspension bridges because they require fewer cables.

Cable-stayed bridges also cost less to build. Their cables are built out only from the towers. In a suspension bridge, the cables are strung across the entire length of the bridge. The financial advantages of cable-stayed bridges have **contributed** to their growing popularity in the United States.

Act Like a Bridge

How does a cable-stayed bridge work? Exactly how do the towers hold up the roadway? If you want an answer to these questions, try acting like a cable-stayed bridge!

Here's what you need to do. Find a partner and two pieces of rope. One piece of rope should be about 5 feet long and the other about 6 feet long. Raise your arms out to the sides of your body, parallel to the floor. Have your partner tie each end of the 5-foot rope around each of your elbows. (Be sure the knots aren't too tight!) Next, drape the middle of the rope over the top of your head. Then, have your partner attach the 6-foot rope to each of your wrists. (Again, be sure the knots aren't too tight.) Finally, drape the second rope over the top of your head.

Notice how your head supports the weight of your arms. Your head is like a bridge tower, your arms are like a roadway, and the ropes are like bridge cables. The rope transfers the weight of your arms to your head, just as the cables on a cable-stayed bridge transfer the weight of the roadway to the towers.

Finally, drop your arms and untie the ropes. Pause for a few moments to appreciate the **ingenious** design of cable-stayed bridges like the beautiful Sunshine Skyway.

CHAPTER 6

Futuristic Bridges

It is likely that bridges built in the future will be different from today's bridges. How will bridges of the future be different? The answer is **incomplete** at present. However, scientific research will certainly determine how bridges change. Researchers will probably develop new building materials and methods. As a result, bridge building will enter new **phases** of safety and economy.

You have learned that bridge engineers are constantly working to improve the strength and **durability** of bridges. Engineers also try to make bridges ever taller, longer, and more beautiful. Their efforts will probably also result in amazing changes in bridges.

You have seen that outside factors, such as the geography of an area and its weather, play a major role in bridge **design**. Forces within bridges also play a role. All these factors determine the best bridge **design** for a particular location.

No one can control the weather or natural events such as earthquakes. However, engineers can control and improve tests on bridges, such as the ones used to test earthquake resistance. As engineers develop better tests, they will begin to introduce new and improved bridge-building **specifications**.

Let's take a close look at a truly awesome bridge. This bridge was built using some recent advances in bridge design and construction methods.

A Record Breaker

The Akashi Kaikyo Bridge soars over the blue waters of the Akashi Strait between Kobe and Awaji-shima Island, Japan. It is an engineering marvel that tested the **ingenuity** and courage of its master bridge builders. What makes this bridge so unusual?

The Akashi Kaikyo Bridge holds many records. It is the world's longest suspension bridge. Its total length is about 13,000 feet. That is almost 2.5 miles! This distance greatly surpasses the length of the previous record holder. That was the 7,283-foot Humber Bridge in England. You'd need four Brooklyn Bridges laid end to end to equal the length of the Akashi Kaikyo Bridge! Its 928-foot towers are the tallest bridge towers in the world.

There are yet more amazing facts about this bridge. The Akashi Kaikyo uses about 190,000 miles of cable. That's enough cable to go around Earth seven times! It cost $4.3 billion to build, which makes it the most expensive suspension bridge ever built.

Aside from its many records, there is another reason for regarding the Akashi Kaikyo as a **monumental** achievement. The builders needed to overcome many **intricate** problems to complete the bridge. The Akashi Kaikyo is in an area of high earthquake activity, hurricanes, typhoons, and gigantic ocean waves called tsunamis. The bridge's foundation had to be constructed in seawater that was up to 360 feet deep. A powerful ocean current flows through the Akashi Strait at a rate of 13 feet per second. There was also a lot of shipping activity to consider. About 1,400 vessels pass through the strait every day. All these factors added up to a first-class bridge-building challenge!

Engineers who worked on the Akashi Kaikyo Bridge were aware of the pitfalls of building long-span bridges. They applied their knowledge to make sure that past bridge-building mistakes weren't repeated. The engineers couldn't have known, however, how soon their expertise would be put to a **monumental** test.

A Super-Sized Job

The Akashi Kaikyo took ten years to complete. Work began in 1988 and ended in 1998. You might think this is a long time to build a bridge. Consider, however, the great size and weight of individual parts of the bridge.

Each of the anchorages at either end of the bridge weighs an incredible 350,000 tons. The two towers are a hefty 23,000 tons each. The total weight of the cables is 57,700 tons. Just moving these materials to the building site in the Akashi Strait was a huge effort.

The first building **phase** involved installing piers, or supports, for the main towers. The piers bear the weight of the bridge towers. Each pier is about 260 feet in diameter.

Hollow structures called caissons were used to create the piers underwater. Six tugboats were needed to pull each enormous caisson to the building site! When the caissons were submerged and in place, they were filled with a new kind of concrete, developed especially for the bridge. This concrete will not disintegrate in water.

The Akashi Kaikyo Bridge in Japan

An Earthshaking Challenge

In 1995, construction on the Akashi Kaikyo was nearing completion. The foundations, towers, and cables were in place. Then, the unexpected happened. On January 17, 1995, the deadly Kobe Earthquake struck. The earthquake registered 7.2 on the Richter scale, which means the earthquake was severe. The quake caused massive destruction. Five thousand people died, mostly in the city of Kobe. This tragedy shocked the world. Japan had seemed so well prepared for earthquakes.

The Akashi Kaikyo did not completely escape the earthquake. The quake moved the towers a little further apart. This stretched the bridge by about 3 feet, so the bridge is a little longer than it was designed to be. Fortunately, the bridge was built to withstand a very powerful quake.

Passing the Test

The engineers of the Akashi Kaikyo Bridge had prepared for an earthquake. They conducted **intricate** earthquake tests on models of the bridge. They used a high-tech device called a shake table. A shake table is a movable concrete table that creates the conditions of earthquakes of different intensities. A shake table can move horizontally and vertically. It can also roll back and forth, rock from side to side, and twist.

The engineers also used wind tunnel testing to determine how wind resistant the bridge was. They used a model of the Akashi Kaikyo Bridge that was 1/100 of the bridge's true size. The model was tested repeatedly to insure that the actual bridge would withstand the ferocious winds in the Akashi Strait. Akashi Kaikyo's builders also protected the bridge **sufficiently** from wind by installing devices called tuned mass dampers (TMDs). TMDs help control the vibrations caused by strong winds.

Like the needle on a sundial, the tower of the Sundial Bridge in Redding, California, casts a long shadow.

Visions of the Future

What will bridges of the future look like? Perhaps the Sundial Bridge in Redding, California, provides some clues. The Sundial Bridge opened on July 4, 2004. It is a pedestrian walkway over the Sacramento River. A Spanish architect named Santiago Calatrava designed the Sundial Bridge. He has been called "the poet of glass and steel."

The Sundial Bridge is a cable-stayed bridge that has an airy, weightless appearance. The cables are suspended from just one soaring, inclined tower. The single 20-story tower provides **sufficient** support for the entire structure. It also acts as a sundial by casting a shadow on a grassy plaza nearby. At night, the bridge glows from the 210 lights beneath the glass panels that form the walkway.

The Sundial Bridge is more than beautiful, however. It is also environmentally sensitive. The bridge passes over a part of the river where salmon lay their eggs. To protect the salmon, the architect **specified** that the bridge supports should not touch the water.

Stretching the Limits

The government of Italy hopes to build a new bridge. It would span the Straits of Messina between Sicily and the mainland of Italy. The new bridge would become the world's longest single-span suspension bridge. Building a bridge over the Straits of Messina involves overcoming major bridge-building challenges, however. There are intense winds in the area and powerful ocean currents in the strait. Four active earthquake faults run right through the strait!

New technology would be used to solve some of these problems. Bridge **designers** would use new computer modeling programs to create a lighter and stronger bridge. **Designers** would also deal with the dangerous waters of the Messina Strait by building the bridge's support towers on land.

How might bridge-building materials change in the future? Chris Williams and Emma Nsugbe have proposed that bridges will be built from artificial bones. Williams and Nsugbe are architects in England. They believe that the simplicity and strength of bones and skeletons will provide answers to bridge **design** problems. Imaginative ideas like this will probably **contribute** to the construction of some amazing bridges in the future.

As you have seen, bridges have evolved from the rope bridges of prehistory to the **monumental** structures of the present day. The journey from the first rough rope bridges to today's super bridges has not been easy. It has been a journey filled with triumph as well as tragedy. Today, bridges are safer than ever. Yet, engineers who attempt to construct the mind-boggling bridges of the future will need to consider the same forces of nature that our ancestors did long ago.

Glossary

abundant plentiful, ample. **Abundant** can also mean teeming or rich in number. An **abundance** is a plentiful amount.

ambitions strong desires to achieve something. To be **ambitious** means having a strong desire for success or achievement.

collisions direct impacts between two or more moving objects. When something **collides** it meets something else in a direct impact.

conceal to hide or keep out of sight, or to keep secret

contours the surface of a curving form. A **contour** is the outline of a figure or object.

contributed given or supplied, or played a part in making something happen. A **contribution** is an object, service, or idea that has been given for a particular purpose.

decade a period of ten years

decay broken-down or rotten matter. To **decay** means to break down gradually or rot.

declined began a downward movement; became less popular

design to plan something. A **design** is also a detailed sketch or drawing that serves as a plan. A **designer** is a person who creates a plan or visual display.

durable strong and long lasting; able to withstand forces that break down or destroy. **Durability** means the ability to withstand wear and tear.

efficient working with less effort, expense, or waste

enabled to have given power to something so it can work. To **enable** means to give power or opportunity. When someone or something **enables**, it supplies the means to do something or allows it to happen.

functions serves or operates

hazard a source of danger. **Hazardous** means dangerous to living things or the environment.

hypothesized had an idea that will be tested. A **hypothesis** is an idea that will be tested.

incomplete lacking something that makes a thing whole

ingenious having or displaying creativity or imagination. **Ingenuity** means cleverness or the ability to be inventive.

intricate having many complex parts; elaborate

maximum the greatest possible, the largest or highest

monumental hugely impressive; of great importance

necessities things that are required or needed

overwhelming overpowering, having a great effect

perceived understood, or noticed. **Perceptions** are understandings gained from using the senses.

phase a stage in a process

precautions things done before an event to prevent danger

precise clear and definite, with strict limits. Something done **precisely** is done in an exact way.

restraints limitations, things that keep you from doing something. To **restrain** is to hold back or keep from doing something.

specifications detailed statements that describe exactly how something should be built or made. **Specified** means stated something in detail.

sufficient in an amount that is adequate or as much as is needed. **Sufficiently** means well enough or adequately.

variations things made slightly different from something else of the same type

visualized saw a picture in one's mind

Index